Money Talks

THE ULTIMATE COUPLE'S GUIDE TO COMMUNICATING ABOUT MONEY

TALAAT AND TAI MCNEELY

DEDICATION

This book is dedicated to all couples who have a true desire to experience a deeper sense of unity with each other in the area of their finances.

CONTENTS

"Communication is a skill that you can learn. It's like riding a bicycle or typing. If you're willing to work at it, you can rapidly improve the quality of every part of your life."

—Brian Tracy

ACKNOWLEDGMENTS

First and foremost, we would like to thank our Lord and Savior Jesus Christ for granting us the ability to do His will on Earth. We want to express our gratitude to every person who has ever communicated to us their desire to be better stewards of the resources that the Lord has provided because you truly are an inspiration for us to continue in this mission.

1
WHAT WE LEARNED ABOUT MONEY AND MARRIAGE

We started HisandHerMoney.com in 2014 as a platform to share what we've learned through our many years of marriage. Our journey hasn't been perfect because we are not perfect people. We are no different than any other couple reading this and we think sharing our triumphs, as well as our challenges, will allow you to see the tips we're laying out in this book truly work.

A little background about us: We started our marriage weighed down with several types of debt, including a car loan, signature bank loans, payday loans, and credit card debt. Complicating matters was that it was Talaat who brought all of the debt into the relationship, something that was hidden until a few months prior to our wedding. Not only did we have to work on digging our way out of debt, but we also had to work on rebuilding trust and re-opening the lines of communication. With a lot of hard work and sacrifice, we have eliminated every ounce of consumer debt and can proudly say we are debt free! There was nothing easy or magical about the process. It took a great deal of hard work and dedication. It was hard work because in our eyes it was a huge amount of debt that was going to take time and perseverance to make it through.

But one of the biggest tools that we used to pay off our debt was our communication. We used a situation that could have broken us and instead used it to turn toward each other and have difficult conversations that allowed us to get clear on our goals and the steps we needed to take to address our debt.

We want more couples to feel financially free and relieved of the burden that carrying debt places on you. But first you've got to have strong communication skills between the two of you. If you can't talk about your problems, there's no way you can formulate a plan together. Furthermore, there's no way you can stick to that plan if you find your communication skills are lacking.

We wrote this book to help readers learn how to break down all communication barriers and from there, discuss and execute their financial dreams and ambitions. We hope that after reading this book, your finances (and your marriage in general) are greatly enhanced.

TALKING POINTS
Discuss with your partner what you desire to get out of reading this book. What improvements would you like to see take place in your discussions about your finances with each other?

2
WHY COMMUNICATION IS ESSENTIAL

Communication is the key to an enduring relationship. When you're able to have open and honest conversations with your partner, it's easier to navigate through life and troubleshoot those inevitable issues—financial or otherwise—that pop up in every relationship.

It's normal for couples to have disagreements. You're two people with your own views and values who may not agree on every problem you face. The true test of your relationship is not whether you see eye to eye on everything, but how you relate to your partner when you don't.

We've had our share of challenges to work through over the span of our relationship. But what we've always committed to doing is focusing on the problem and not attacking the other person.

Oh, the temptation is there to sling insults at your partner. But what does it solve? When you decide to attack the problem and not your partner, it's easier to get to a solution because you're not weighed down by defensiveness and ego.

If you realize that you are somebody who gets unsettled easily and has a strong temper, you have to practice remaining calm and learn how to "fight fair." Here's some of the tips we've used when our conversations begin to get heated:

Take a breather

Understand no two individuals are the same. Along these lines, you can't hope to change your partner to your fantasy girl or dream guy. They are who they are and you have to roll with the current version of your partner, not who you wish they'd be. So we recommend taking a breather and remembering that you fell in love with your spouse for who they are, not for how often they agree with you.

Listen first

Show of hands: how many of you have been guilty of listening to your partner just long enough so you can formulate a rebuttal? We have definitely been guilty from time to time in our marriage. Figure out how to listen first. And we mean really listen. This helps your partner feel respected and heard, which will help the discussion progress smoothly and fairly.

Be kind before arguments arise

Your day-to-day interaction should be kind and fair. Giving each other compliments and sharing appreciation helps solidify your relationship so when those occasional conflicts arise, you're operating from a place of love. Make a special effort to let your partner know they are loved.

Don't expect them to be a mind-reader

Not only is this completely irrational, it will also cause significant issues. We did this too many times in the beginning of our marriage. I, Tai, would get frustrated because I felt like Talaat should save more money and he felt frustrated because he felt that he worked hard enough to spend his money. We both were walking around frustrated without expressing our feelings to one another. It wasn't until we sat down and had a thorough discussion about our spending and saving habits that we were able to get rid of that frustration.

Let's say you *do* expect your partner to be able to tell what you want and what you mean. After all, you've been together for a while and in that time they should begin to learn more about you and how you see the world, right? Read the following scenario and check whether you can relate:

You need your partner to assist more with tasks around the house. To make your wishes known, you start to make vague remarks to your partner about the condition of the house when you return home: "Wow, those dishes are really piling up in the sink. When's the last time we mopped the kitchen floor?"

Would you expect your partner to hop up and say, "I'll get right to cleaning"? Or would they, most likely, look around and go, "You're right—we do need to clean up" and go right back to whatever they were doing?

Rather than serving hints or making passive aggressive statements, sit down with your partner and clarify what you need. Offer a solution and listen to their thoughts. In the above scenario, maybe the household tasks need to be reconfigured a certain way so both parties come to a happy medium. Or maybe the jobs need to be outsourced through a housekeeping service.

Don't try to "win"

If you're both focused on who "wins," both people wind up losing. Stop concentrating on "me" and instead think about "we."

Mind your "I" statements

"You" statements have a tendency to incite defensive reactions. "I" statements put the emphasis on the speaker rather than the receiver of the message. Read the following statements to see which one sounds more productive:

1) "You're always so forgetful! This is the third time this year we've had to pay a late fee because you forgot to pay a bill. We need to just sign up for automatic bill

payments since I can't trust you to do it."

2) "I would feel better if we took some time to sign up for automatic bill payments for all our utility bills. That way neither one of us has to worry about it and we can relax."

Which did you prefer?

At some point in every relationship, there comes a problem that takes some grit to solve. Again, this isn't a sign that you're incompatible. It simply means you are human. It's up to the two of you to figure out how to work together, respectfully, to solve your problems, including your financial ones.

TALKING POINTS
On a scale from 1 to 10 (10 being the highest), how would you rate your communication currently with your spouse? After reading this book, reflect back to your number and see if you still agree with what you chose.

3
WHY YOU NEED TO TALK ABOUT MONEY

Depending on how each person was raised, there might be hesitation to discuss money issues. But most of the time, the issues that emerge in your marriage are not directly related to money, but instead based on a misconception around how your partner handles money.

As a rule, each person in the relationship might have a different style of managing money. Some are savers and others are spenders. Some are comfortable with carrying a little debt, while others run screaming from owing anyone any amount of money. Some are experts in investing, while others have no desire to deal with an investment portfolio. Some are long-term minded, while their partner wants to live for today. It's rare to find the couple where each partner has the same values and viewpoints on money management. It is more likely for opposites to attract, and that is why many couples find financial issues truly upsetting in marriage.

Communication is the key to figuring out how to mesh different money styles. Even if you're more than a decade into your relationship, it's never too late to get on the same page.

You don't have to completely change your money style. The key is to figure out what benefits your marriage most and allows you to thrive as a couple.

Here are some key questions to begin your conversations about money:

1. What are your spending habits? Do you pay with credit cards or cash? Do you know the amount you spend consistently? How do you track your spending?
2. What do you spend your money on? Do you tend to splurge on big ticket items or are you more inclined to spend frugally?
3. Do you feel comfortable living within your means? Do you purchase things simply because they are on sale? Is it hard to pass up a good deal?
4. Are you a saver or a spender? If you are a saver, what do you do with the money you've saved? Do you invest it? If you are a spender, do you feel comfortable with the amount of money you usually spend?
5. What is your mentality towards debt? Do you know how much debt you have? Do you have credit cards, lines of credit, school loans, etc.? If so, do you have a plan to pay it off?
6. Do you donate to charity or give to your church? Is it something that is a priority to you, no matter how much you earn?
7. How would you feel about joint accounts? Do you want to keep separate records for individual spending?
8. What are your financial objectives and needs? Have you taken the time to write down your financial goals? Does your relationship change any of those objectives?

Keep in mind these questions exist to help you discover one another, not to help you *change* one another. There are no right or wrong answers to these questions. Rather they should set the stage to opening up the lines of communication. All couples will benefit from this exercise. Try it for yourself.

Understanding and fixing money conflicts

Most divorces come down to two issues: sex and money. With the financial side of things, it's easy to see why money complicates relationships to the point where both parties would rather jump ship than try to reach an agreement. Money is extremely personal. And particularly for couples who have lived on their own a few years before getting into the relationship, we tend to get set in our ways and think our way is always the best way to do things.

It takes time to get used to the thought of merging finances and compromising with another flawed human. But there are steps you can take to manage your conflicts without it turning into an all-out war. Here's how to discuss your finances without losing your love for each other:

1. **Let one individual be the leader.** He or she can deal with the checkbook, the budgeting system and take the lead on the financial planning. In our household Tai handles writing the checks and paying the bills. But we both have a say when putting together our monthly budget. One spouse taking the lead does not mean that the other spouse sits back and has no financial involvement.

2. **Review your financial goals quarterly and annually.** Both sides should have a complete comprehension of where money is going, and each person has veto power when it comes to financial planning.

3. **Be adaptable.** Understand that your financial goals may need to shift and unexpected circumstances (home repair bills, car accidents, etc.) may cause a bit of a financial headache. Be flexible and remember that as long as you operate as a team, nothing can stop you!

4. **Don't hold grudges.** At the point when one of you overspends, spends rashly, or doesn't spend enough

(and it will happen), don't let those negative feelings linger. Instead, have a level-headed conversation about the problem and make changes so both of you feel good moving forward.

Maintaining a good marriage is tough. Maintaining a good marriage, while trying to wisely handle your money, is even tougher. We have found that there are some very common mistakes that many couples make in regards to how they approach their finances.

Mistake #1: Lack of honesty

Too often we are not always fully forthright with our significant others when it comes to the total picture of our financial situation. At times, we may elect to be somewhat elusive with our spouse in regards to issues such as our spending habits, or the amount of debt that we have accumulated. Being anything less than open and honest with each other when it comes to how you each are dealing with money, will produce nothing but disastrous results for your marriage.

Honesty is the best policy, especially when it comes to the handling of your money. Marriage and money are challenging areas in our lives by themselves, and when you combine the two the challenge becomes even greater.

Therefore, it's imperative that we are fully open and that we discuss current debt loads and spending tendencies with each other. This is important so that once each of you lays all of your cards on the table, collectively you can come up with a game plan to move forward in your finances TOGETHER!

Mistake #2: Lack of communication

Communication is more than just simply speaking with each other. It involves listening, just as much as it does talking. Couples must communicate about their money in order to ensure that positive momentum is being made, and that you are both pushing in the same direction. One of the primary vehicles in which couples should communicate about their finances is through a budget. (We will discuss this more in Chapter 7.)

Consistent communication about your money is a surefire way to achieve the financial independence that each of us is striving for.

Mistake #3: Lack of accountability

When couples lack accountability in their finances, it leaves room for nothing but catastrophic consequences to manifest themselves.

Accountability is not a means for one spouse to control the other. When used properly, being accountable helps each of you to focus and stay the course in your journey to gain and maintain control of your finances.

Set spending boundaries and then lovingly help each other to stay within the means that you've collectively set for yourselves.

Putting it all together

As the old saying goes, "Teamwork makes the dream work." Your spouse is your teammate! Teams that maintain open and honest communication and consistently remain accountable to each other, tend to win championships.

If you and your spouse want to win with your money, then work diligently to avoid these three mistakes at all costs. In doing so, you will be more than on your way to financial freedom.

Don't let money push you apart. Use it to bring you together and to create a brighter tomorrow.

TALKING POINTS

Money conflicts will arise. When they do, make sure you address them right away. We like to call a meeting where we each take turns and discuss a resolution. Is there anything that you would like to share with your spouse after reading this chapter? Now is the time to do it!

4
WHEN COUPLES SHOULD HAVE THE MONEY TALK

The timetable for the money discussion is going to be different for every couple. We don't recommend bringing up the issue on the first date, yet it's unlikely you'd wait years before you see if you can mesh financially with your partner.

It is easier to have the discussion sooner rather than later. It is something that should be at the foundation of your relationship.

Simply put, money makes the world go round. The majority of your life decisions—where you work, live, eat, and invest your spare time—will revolve around how much is in your bank account and how the two of you view money. The relationship we have with our money is forever, and you would be wise to be in agreement with your partner.

Here are six types of financial discussions to have with a significant other:

1. How will we earn money? This question is designed to have you discuss what your career goals are. Are you looking to rise high in your field, leading to long nights and frequent work travel? Are you content

with a middle-of-the-road job and salary, allowing you flexibility with your family? Do either of you have strong feelings about one parent staying at home to take care of the kids?

2. How will we spend our money? Do we want to buy a home, travel, go back to school? What are some of those line items that need to be in our budget? Would you be comfortable agreeing to check in with your partner before making a purchase over a certain amount?

3. How will you both stay informed concerning your cash and total assets? Will you keep a financial plan? Who will pay the bills?

4. How will we save money? Do we plan to have an emergency fund? How much do we want to save monthly? Are there any financial savings goals that we want to reach?

5. Are we going to invest or start a business? Knowing one another's risk tolerance level is imperative.

6. What type of legacy are we trying to build? What quality of life would you like to have when you retire?

It is possible to discover all the answers to these questions just by observing your partner over time. However, if you are serious about building a life together (and that means merging finances), it's crucial to be open and honest about your financial goals and try to get in the same chapter (not necessarily on the same page!).

TALKING POINTS

If you're engaged or in a serious relationship, start to discuss your money habits. If you are married and have never had an in-depth talk about your money, start now using the questions in this chapter.

5
SPENDERS AND SAVERS UNITE

Most of the couples we know have one thing in common: one is a saver and the other is a spender. And we were no different.

> **Talaat:** "When I was younger, the lessons on earning money and spending money went hand in hand. There have been plenty of times where my money was already spent mentally, before I even got the paycheck physically."

> **Tai:** "I come from a family of five children, so growing up, I was always conscious about how money was spent. I am very conscious of how I spend and save money to this very day."

One of our first big challenges was the discovery of Talaat's debt. While he had made strides to clean up his credit and eliminate his debt, it took time to understand how we could work together to solve this dilemma.

We believe our story is proof that spenders and savers can

indeed work together and have a solid relationship without a lot of financial turmoil. Do you know which category you fall into?

You are most likely a spender if you do most of the following:
- Swipe your debit/credit card without knowing if you have enough to cover the charge.
- Must have the latest and newest gadgets that come out.
- Never reconcile your expenses or receipts.
- Shop to fill a void or to make yourself feel happy.
- Every time someone invites you out to dinner or on a trip, you are there.

You are most likely a saver if you do most of the following:
- Know how much you have in your account before you swipe your debit/credit card
- Wear clothing and shoes until they just about fall apart.
- Budget for major purchases before going out to buy it.
- Never shop without going to the clearance section or having a coupon first.
- Consider yourself a homebody and regularly say no to dinner or vacation invites.

Now these questions in and of themselves are not a surefire way to know if you are a saver or a spender. However, if you look at yourself and begin to be honest, you can just about answer the question without any doubt.

First, we have to think about how a saver might be attracted to a spender and vice versa. A saver may appear to be sensible and reasonable, which speaks to the spender. A spender may appear fun and unconstrained to a saver. It goes back to "opposites attract."

At first, all might be well in the relationship as you balance each other out. But as the relationship gets stronger and the finances begin to merge, what initially attracted you to your partner ("She's so good with her money!") might be the thing that turns you off ("She's so cheap!").

Consequently, it's important that you learn to manage these different financial styles for your relationship to thrive. This is why so many premarital workshops and marriage enhancement classes now focus on helping couples problem-solve this very common conundrum.

Let's take a look at how this spender/saver match might play out in a normal circumstance: arranging a vacation.

To begin with, it may never occur to the saver to even take a break from work. If not for their spender companion reminding him/her to rest and energize, he or she may go years without a vacation on the grounds that "getting away from it all" drains your bank account. Furthermore, if the saver does consider taking some time off, the plans might get buried in exploration: "If I'm going to take a trip, I better make sure I get the best deal possible." Subsequently, they may spend weeks on Kayak or TripAdvisor trying to make sure they don't pay a penny more than they need to.

Then again, spenders regularly push to gain experiences, have a great time and appreciate the rewards for so much hard work. In contrast to the saver, a spender may hear about a fantastic resort and book that getaway on the spot.

This is where it can get tricky. Rather than the saver seeing his spender wife as adding satisfaction and fervor to his life, he sees her as being reckless and flighty. Rather than the spender seeing her saver spouse as too intentioned and wary, she sees him as exhausting and modest. The truth is that when they cooperate, they get what's best for one another and for the relationship.

Taking the case somewhat further, envision that you two actually do take the vacation. Now you have to choose if and when you'll go out to eat. The saver may argue that it's best to get a hotel room with a kitchenette so you can heat up some pasta for supper. In the saver's eyes, not going out to eat means freeing up more money to do other things. Then again, the spender may want to eat out for each meal, saying, "If we have a couple of days for vacation, we should capitalize on those hours by not slaving over a stove or eating PB&Js."

Both parties sound reasonable, right? It's about understanding where the other person is coming from and working together to come up with a solution. In the above scenario, perhaps a compromise could be selecting a hotel that offers a free breakfast, thus eliminating costs for at least one meal per day.

It is not always easy to mesh different financial styles, but it is possible. Use the following tips to make your spender/saver love work:

- See the benefits in your partner's financial views. If you're a spender, isn't it nice that your partner is diligent about avoiding late fees? Or savers, isn't it wonderful that your partner will not hesitate to celebrate your accomplishments with a night on the town?
- Discuss money issues while you're calm and relaxed. Timing is everything.
- No name-calling. If you don't care for the way your partner is acting, ask questions to get to the bottom of the situation: "Is there a reason you don't think we should take a family vacation this summer?"
- Always look for the compromise. If you stay level-headed and open-minded, you can usually find one.

TALKING POINTS
Tell your spouse whether you consider yourself a spender or a saver and see if they agree. Then discuss how you all can play to each other's financial strengths in order to begin winning with your money.

6

THE BREADWINNER BATTLE AND
TWO-INCOME TRAP

According to the most recent data from the U.S. Bureau of Labor Statistics, nearly 30 percent of wives now make more than their husbands.

While most men would be thrilled to see their partner excelling at work and bringing home a hefty salary, some men are still uncomfortable when their wife outearns them. Traditionally, these men have taken pride in their role as a provider, and having a wife that can make a bigger contribution can be seen as a threat to his place in the family. On the flip side, some of these breadwinning women feel uncomfortable or guilty when they out-earn their husbands.

Don't let money demolish your marriage; instead, use this opportunity to discuss how this situation can bring you closer. This is where teamwork comes into play. As two people working on the same side, who makes more shouldn't be a primary concern. Financially, you're in this together.

For men

See her accomplishments as something worth being thankful for and be cheerful for her, bolster her and appreciate what you have together.

For women

Let your partner know he is still cherished and acknowledged for what he accomplishes for the family. His value goes far beyond what he brings home financially.

Beware of the two-income trap

Society has wrongly programmed us into thinking that we need two incomes in a household to thrive. That's simply not true! You should never base your financial situation off of both your and your spouse's income. As a matter of fact, you should live off of just one of your incomes. What we mean by this is, you should make all of your major financial decisions based on one of your salaries.

You should never purchase your home based of two incomes, and most definitely not your vehicles. Not even your children's daycare tuition, or utility bills. You may say, "Well, in that case we won't be able to live at all." We beg to differ! If you base all of your major financial necessities off of one income, you won't be living above your means. We did just that midway into our marriage.

Avoiding the trap

We made the conscious decision to live off one income alone. We took into consideration the possibility that one day, becoming a stay-at-home mom could be a reality. Another question that we posed to ourselves was, what if one of us gets laid off from our job? We did not want to be stretched thin financially. If we did, we knew we would be placing ourselves on the brink of losing everything because of a lifestyle that was built on the basis of having two incomes.

By doing this, we were able to use the other person's income to do more meaningful things. For example, we used the second income to purchase an investment property. This is something that we never would have been able to do, if we needed both of our incomes to make ends meet. We were able to jump into the investment world with both feet, without being afraid. We also gave more to our local church, as well as to people who were in need. Additionally, we went on family vacations and even dined out at a few fancy places from time to time. Most importantly, we were able to continuously add to our growing savings account!

Decisions decisions

Our diligence was put to the test by the time we had our second child. I decided to come home and stay with our children. It started to become really challenging juggling work schedules, childcare, dinner, and all of the millions of obligations that come with being a career woman. So for me, the best thing to do was to come home full time. As it turned out, this actually became an easy transition for me. What made the transition smooth was the fact that we had already established a standard of living that did not involve my income. As a matter of fact, we purchased a larger home for our growing family. By God's grace, we were able to do so strictly on my husband's income!

How many people are working because they absolutely have to, at a job that they absolutely hate? If we would have based all of our financial needs off both of our incomes, I would not have been able to follow my heart's desire and come home full time with our children. It brings me so much joy when I can take our children to school, without thinking about impending bills to pay based on me working. It's something that you can get used to very quickly. We would not have been able to do this if we did not budget our life based solely on one income!

Try it out for yourself

Doing a budget every month has allowed us to live off one income effectively. Give it a try for yourselves. If you are in a household with two incomes, take the next couple of months and put it to the test. Make all of your financial decisions based off one of your salaries. You may have to cut back on some things to make it work. However, you will quickly find out that it's simply the best way for you to establish your lifestyle. Nobody knows what's ahead down the road. Nevertheless, we can all plan for our future in the best way that we know how.

TALKING POINTS

Is it a problem if she makes more in the relationship? Ask them how they feel. Do you belittle your partner if he/she makes less than you? Do you think you could try to live off one income for the next few months?

7
HOW TO TALK ABOUT YOUR BUDGET

Couples must communicate about their money in order to ensure that positive momentum is being made, and that you are both pushing in the same direction. One of the primary vehicles in which couples should communicate about their finances is through a monthly budget.

Budgets serve as road maps to allow each of you to have a clear view as to what money is coming in and how you plan to spend it. You wouldn't take a family road trip from New York to California without first mapping out the journey. By mapping out the journey, you have a clear understanding of what roads you need to take in order to reach your ultimate destination.

Your budget is no different, in that it serves as the GPS for your financial journey from month to month. It allows you both to have a concrete plan. This will allow you to reach your desired destination in the area of your finances.

The whole point of budgeting is to give yourself control over where your money is going. This does not mean that you have to take all of the fun things that you are accustomed to doing out of your lifestyle. It's actually quite the contrary. Budgeting gives you the power to shape and mold your monthly income in a way that makes sense for you financially, socially, and personally. It turned out to be a real turning point in our journey to becoming debt free.

The starting point

The first thing that you have to do is figure out how much money you're spending. Spend the first 30 days tracking all of your expenses. A good tip would be to keep a little notebook, or a checkbook register with you at all times. That way, every time you make a purchase you can just jot it down on the spot, so that you don't forget later. This gives you a baseline. When you formulate your budget you have an idea of how much money you have been spending in each category of your budget. After the 30 days are up, you now have a clear picture as to where your money has been going. This information will allow you to make adjustments moving forward. In addition, we also recommend you look at your last two bank statements to get a better idea of your money habits, expenses and income.

The formulation of your budget always begins with the amount of income that you bring home every month. Once you have established how much your take home pay is, you can come up with a plan to allocate each and every dollar out of your income to a specific category. You have to prioritize what you need to spend your money on first. Your first obligation should be to take care of the "four walls" of your home. Start by budgeting for your mortgage/rent, real estate taxes, utilities, food, and basic clothing, and then work your way down from there.

Keep it real

Remember to be conservative and realistic, when deciding how much money you want to allocate in each spending category. You don't want to overcompensate in one area of your budget if it will leave you short in another area. For example, having $200 allocated for entertainment is not a good idea if that only leaves you with $50 to eat for the rest of the month.

In order for your budget to be successful, make sure that you include a category for everything that you spend money on in a given month. This includes childcare, medications, cell phone bills, trips to the hair salon, EVERYTHING! You will be able to use the information that you wrote down during your 30-day trial period to base your numbers on. Put the appropriate amount of money in each category that you think you need to survive on. Your budget is your guide; it is there to help you move through the month with a foolproof plan to spend your money, instead of getting to the end of the month wondering how it all disappeared.

This budgeting concept is not easy at first, but it is well worth it in the end. Your first month will be difficult. You will not get it 100 percent correct on the first try. It's much like riding a bicycle for the first time— you will probably fall off a couple times before you master it. The same can be said for your budget. Your first couple of attempts will be rough. But if you stick with it you will become a master, and it will become just another part of your everyday life.

Discover a great money manager

The biggest misconception about money management is that somehow your finances will work themselves out without any effort from you. Clearly this isn't the case. That is why it is crucial that you make a game plan for your money. If you don't quite feel comfortable going at it alone, one option is to hire a financial advisor. As an objective third-party, they can help you create a suitable budget and also give insight on the best ways to save, invest, and grow your money. Yet if you do work with a financial advisor, you should still be an active participant in your own finances.

Plan financial conferences

Set a date with your partner where the two of you will sit down together and discuss your financial plan before the month begins. Make these gatherings intriguing and fun; doing stuff to lighten the atmosphere will make these exchanges lovely and beneficial. We like to make a nice hot cup of tea and eat our favorite snack while discussing our financial future together!

Create financial objectives and budget

Considering each person's desires as you work on your budget is key, especially if your financial styles differ. Each person will have to give a little to compromise and come up with the best budget for the relationship.

Carry out the budget

One particular financial system we like to use is the envelope system. Every month we take out cash for certain categories in our budget and put the cash in individual envelopes. Each cash category has its own envelope, with a starting balance.

As the month goes by and we use cash for whatever reason, we write down where, when and how much we spent. This allows us to keep a running balance, so we know where we stand at any given time during the month. You can use regular white mailing envelopes or a small coupon file accordion.

Budgeting your monthly finances does not have to be cumbersome, and it doesn't have to cost you any money. Every single resource that we have outlined below is 100% FREE, so there is no reason for you not to create your budget right away. By using some of the resources that we have listed below, you can save yourself time and money.

BudgetSimple

BudgetSimple.com is a free budgeting and personal finance tool that focuses on making sure you have a budget that works for you. BudgetSimple aims to make the process as easy and approachable as possible and promises that an hour with the tool will give you a better understanding of where your money is going. Once you have your budget and you're all set up, it's a matter of keeping your finances in check, and the tool helps you with that as well. BudgetSimple is completely free, but if you want the mobile app or the option to fully link your bank accounts, there is a fee for their premium account.

Mint

Mint.com was one of the first free, web-based personal finance tools to plug in to all of your bank accounts, investments, retirement funds, credit cards, and other financial accounts to quickly give you a complete picture of your financial health. Mint also lets you draw up a household budget (with warnings if you're not sticking to it), track your spending, set savings goals, and actually stick to them. Mint doesn't touch your money itself—it just uses read-only access to show you everything—but it does suggest financial products that might save you money in the long run, like lower-interest credit cards or higher-interest savings accounts.

Buxfer

Buxfer.com is another popular budget-management tool. Like Mint, it provides income and account information, online security and budget/spending categories. Buxfer's site is user-friendly and well-designed, and it features a free, live demo. Buxfer specializes in budgeting and tracking group expenses. This simple online money management service allows users the cool features of tracking loans and IOUs from friends and family as well as providing group budgeting. They offer three packages: a free basic version that is limited to five accounts and budgets, and a plus and pro version that are fee-based accounts that come with other features such as unlimited accounts, advance reports, online payments and more.

Budget Pulse

BudgetPulse.com is for the security conscious and it's also free. This budgeting tool doesn't require users to input their banking account information for tracking, and lets users manually enter or import their banking data from computer files. Another great feature is that BudgetPulse allows users to set up budgeting and saving goals.

There is also a really cool social networking aspect to this tool, because it allows users to publicize their goals (if they so choose) to friends and family, who can then contribute to a goal through PayPal or just cheer you on and congratulate you.

Budget Tracker

BudgetTracker.com specializes in tracking transactions, with or without a link to your bank account information.

The unique feature to this one is the ability to customize applications on the site, creating more areas for the tool to track and letting you choose what to display from dates and titles to amounts and more specific details.

The results from the tracking are shown on your calendar and in graphs on the site. You can even use other applications created by other users on the site. Forecasting outcomes, scheduling income dates, and various business-based features are available.

moneyStrands

Like the other tools, moneyStrands.com can help you visualize your bill payments and spending on its calendars, bar graphs, and more. However, this budgeting tool focuses more on financial planning than on tracking transactions. It can still automatically track your expenses by linking the service to your bank accounts, but moneyStrands goes further by generating budgets based on spending habits, along with generating personal financial tips for each user.

TALKING POINTS

Do you currently operate your household on a budget? If not, identify a tool that you will use to begin the budgeting process. That could be a website like the ones we've mentioned or just a simple Microsoft Excel spreadsheet. Remember that both parties have to participate in the process to avoid resentment building up in your relationship. Discuss each category of the budget and listen to each other's opinions.

8
HOW TO TALK ABOUT YOUR DEBT

For most couples, having some degree of debt is a given. Whether it's student loans, credit cards, car payments, or maybe even a mortgage, debt is something that will require both people to be on the same page to tackle.

Ideally, the debt discussion should take place before the wedding. After you get hitched, "his or her debt" becomes "our debt," so it's best for each partner to know what they're signing up for.

That was one of our biggest financial challenges as a couple. Only months away from saying "I do," some financial discoveries were made that rocked us to our core:

Talaat: "My gut instinct told me not to tell Tai about the debt that I was bringing into our marriage because I didn't want her to view me differently. So I went on this feverish plan to get rid of the debt on my own so I didn't have to bring anything into the marriage. But it didn't work, so I had to admit that I had not been truthful."

Tai: "I started to doubt and question everything. When I

found out he was still carrying a lot of debt, I was devastated. What hurt me the most was the trust was gone. How could I believe anything he told me after that?"

We learned that you must be truthful no matter what. Even though it's scary to talk about some of the ways you may have been irresponsible in the past, don't lie to your spouse. It's only going to make things worse.

Here are a few suggestions we have for couples beginning to talk about debt, based on our personal experience:

- **Commit to transparency.** The only way to ensure that you both can trust each other financially is to commit to a relationship that is based on transparency. This means no secret or hidden purchases or moving money around to cover your tracks.
- **Develop a plan of action.** Together, the two of you can put together a plan to attack the debt, determining how quickly you can get rid of it.
- **Stick together.** In a case like ours, where one person held all the debt, it could have been easy for Tai to get upset at this "extra" work to rebuild their finances. But because Tai knew that Talaat was working just as hard, if not harder, to eliminate his debt, she was able to remain an encouraging partner.

Getting out of debt can sometimes be a daunting task. However, once you start thinking differently when it comes to your mindset about debt, you will win! You have to first take the necessary steps to learn as much as you can about what got you in this place. We have compiled a list of eight steps that will lead you on your way to financial freedom! We can attest to each of these steps, because it's what we did to become victorious over our money.

1. Lay all cards on the table.

Debt elimination begins with you taking inventory of exactly how much you owe, to whom, and at what interest rates. Write down all of your balances, with their respective interest rates.

It's very beneficial to know what your minimum payments are, for every account. After tracking down all of your debts, you'll have a decent idea of how much is owed. Take a long hard look at your list of debts, and marinate on it.

You now have a clear picture of the hole that you need to dig out of. Don't let worry and despair creep in. Now is not the time to worry about past mistakes. Now is the time to keep your thoughts on your future.

2. Get your mind right.

When getting out of debt, it's important to have the proper mentality. You cannot be cool with your debt; you have to view it as an enemy to your future. Debt elimination is a tough process that requires you to have a disciplined mindset to accomplish it.

In his classic book, *The 7 Habits of Highly Effective People*, Stephen R. Covey tells his readers to always "begin with the end in mind." That simply means that at the very beginning of your debt elimination process, you have to stay focused on the finish line to be successful.

By allowing your mind to be focused on the end result (being debt free), the distractions that will arise will not detour you from your mission. In this way, you are taking responsibility, and maintaining laser focus on your ultimate goal. Get rid of any "stinking thinking," and get your mind right for the task at hand.

3. Make a written plan.

Once you get your mind right, it's time to take action and write out your plan. It's time to do the math and put the numbers on paper. Developing a budget that tracks your income and expenses is crucial to getting out of debt in a short period of time. It will help you gauge where you are with your finances, so that you can move forward toward your goal.

Go over each item on your budget, and decrease any bill that you can. It may involve cancelling services that you rarely use, like a gym membership, or downgrading your cable bill. It might even involve reducing the number of times that you dine out at restaurants each month. The amount that you slash depends upon your commitment level to getting out of debt.

The more committed you are, the easier it will be for you to give up some of the unnecessary luxuries of life. You might not even need to sacrifice that much if you can find these items or services for less.

When making your budget, it's important to get on the same page with your spouse. If you are married, then getting out of debt is a joint project. To make it through, both parties must be working together, on the same page, and communicating effectively.

4. Decide to stop borrowing money.

If you want to get out of debt fast, you have to stop using debt to fuel your lifestyle. No longer will you be financing furniture, signing up for credit cards, or test driving brand new cars that you can't pay for in cash.

This will help you focus solely on the debt that you currently have, so that you can develop a game plan to pay it off quickly. Acquiring more debt will only keep you drowning in the same bills that you keep saying you want to eliminate.

5. Create a small emergency fund.

When you start the process of getting out of debt, you can be sure that some type of money sucking event will take place. A tire will blow out, your water heater will stop working, or you'll get a speeding ticket out of nowhere. Trust us, something will come up.

Having money set to aside specifically for these unforeseen events will prevent you from incurring more debt to fix the situation. The ideal emergency fund can vary depending upon your income. Ideally, it's best to aim for a minimum of $500 to $1,000.

When you are trying to get out of debt, you need to put a buffer between you and your debt. By creating a small emergency fund for yourself, you are doing exactly that.

6. Attack debt smallest to largest.

Line up all of your debts, from smallest to largest. Financial guru Dave Ramsey coined this strategy as the "Snowball Method." In this technique, you make the minimum payments on all of your accounts. You then focus on one debt at a time from smallest to largest.

You send any and every extra penny that you can carve out of your budget, and you apply it to the smallest debt; not the debt with the highest interest rate. After you pay off the smallest debt, you then apply that same payment as an additional payment on the next smallest debt.

Use momentum to snowball from one success to the next. Use precision and acceleration when attacking each debt. Remember to focus all your energy on one debt at a time, from smallest to largest. This goes against the conventional idea of paying your debt from highest interest rate to lowest interest rate. However, we have personally found that getting that first small victory lights a heck of a fire underneath you to finish the race.

7. Sell your stuff.

Sell anything that serves as a stumbling block. Excess clutter, gadgets, and items that you're just not using anymore may actually be inhibiting spiritual growth and freedom. By relieving yourself of the excess in your house, there's not only extra money to apply to your debt, but you also gain a feeling of solace.

Gather up everything that you don't absolutely need, and list it at reasonable prices on websites like eBay, Craigslist, and even Facebook. Remember these are mostly used items, so don't try and sell them at retail prices. The key is to get rid of things you don't need to have some cash to pile onto your debt.

8. Give and serve.

On the journey to becoming debt free, you may find yourself becoming a tightwad with your money. This is a tendency that we want you to avoid at all cost.

We've always been givers, even when we were in debt. Your journey to financial freedom is not the time to stop giving. In fact, giving wisely can welcome opportunities, relationships and other blessings into your life.

Giving does not always need to be in the financial sense. It might mean giving of your time or your skills. When done with good intentions, this extra service will be the real key to your financial freedom in the end.

TALKING POINTS
Identify how much debt you are in. Find out the balances, minimum payments, and interest rate of all of your debts. Discuss a plan of action to attack your debt, and then execute. Be open and allow each other to lay it all out on the table. Create an atmosphere for honesty and transparency. It is very difficult for a spouse to open up and become vulnerable and discuss their financial failures with their spouse, if they are afraid of the outcome.

9
HOW TO TALK ABOUT YOUR FINANCIAL GOALS

Setting financial goals can be difficult for couples, particularly when two individuals have different mindsets about money. You probably won't ever see eye to eye on everything, but it's important to begin with a healthy level of respect and open-mindedness.

We believe that it is a great tool for couples to build a unified and meaningful relationship. Creating goals together inspires you to dare to accomplish higher heights together as a team. It stimulates conversations for you both to see yourselves, not just for where you are, but for where you want to go.

Goal setting is a practice that should be done as a team. If you are not currently married, or in a relationship, then find a trustworthy accountable partner to assist you in the process. For couples, it's imperative that you create goals collectively. Creating goals together will help you to continue to support each other in the accomplishment of your dreams.

There is no greater support that you can have than that of

the person that you love. In order for you both to properly support each other, you each need to have a clear understanding of the goals that you want to achieve.

We have always made it a point to share our individual goals with each other. Additionally, we collectively make goals that we want to achieve together.

In your journey towards financial independence, setting and accomplishing financial goals has to become a part of your mission. You both should sit down and assess your current situation together, and establish goals from there. In order for goal setting to be effective, you need to have a clear picture of your current state first.

First you must write your goals down. A goal that is not written down is nothing more than an idea. The Bible also supports this notion in Habakkuk 2:2, which states:

...Write the vision, and make it plain...

Keep in mind that when writing your goals, you can't write them in just any old way. As you are writing down your financial goals, you need to make sure they're SMART: *specific, measurable, attainable, realistic,* and *time-bound.* Let's break each of these principles down to gain a better understanding of them:

SPECIFIC

Your financial goals must be clear and distinct. When your goals are specific, you know exactly what is expected, when, and how much. It's not good enough to simply set a goal of, "I plan to get out of debt." That is way too ambiguous. Instead, be specific and say, "I plan to eliminate my $12,000 student loan debt that I owe to Sallie Mae within the next 18 months." Because the goals are specific, you can easily measure your progress toward their completion.

MEASURABLE

If your financial goals are not measurable, you will never know whether you're making progress toward their successful completion. It will become difficult for you to stay motivated to complete your goals when you have no milestones to indicate their progress. So if you have a goal to increase your net worth by $10,000 within the next 12 months, break that number down into $2,000 milestones to track your progress.

ATTAINABLE

Financial goals must be realistic and attainable for you to reach. The best goals will require you to stretch out to achieve them, but they aren't extreme. The goals are neither out of reach, nor too easy to attain. For instance, if your income is $50,000 annually, then don't set a goal to pay off your $200,000 mortgage in the next six months. That is not really an attainable goal, based on your current financial situation.

Conversely, if you have an annual income of $100,000, don't set a goal of paying off a $500 credit card balance over the next 12 months. Goals that are set too high or too low become meaningless, and you will naturally begin to ignore them.

RELEVANT

Your goals must be relevant to what you want to achieve financially, in the short and long term. Where do you want to be financially 6, 12, 18 months from now? Furthermore, what do you want your financial picture to look like 5 to 10 years from now? Create your financial goals with these benchmarks in mind.

Understanding your future financial picture is critical in this respect. Sometimes, you can be tempted to do something simply because it is easy and sounds great, only to discover later, that it has no long-term importance to what you want to achieve, as an individual or a couple.

TIME-BOUND

Goals must have starting points, ending points, and fixed durations. Committing yourself to deadlines will help you focus all efforts on completion of the goal, on or before its due date.

Financial goals without deadlines tend to be overtaken by the day-to-day issues that will invariably arise in your lives.

TALKING POINTS

Keep a journal and jot down your goals and ambitions and talk about them to each other. Do you want to start a business one day? How about go on a dream vacation? Write down these goals and post them in a prominent location in your home so that you are able to refer back to them. We suggest revisiting your goals every quarter as well as annually.

10
KEEPING EACH OTHER ACCOUNTABLE

We've talked briefly about accountability in an earlier chapter, but we think it's so crucial that it deserves its own section.

Let's be honest: sometimes working hard on your financial goals can feel stifling. You might feel like you work hard, so you should be able to spend your money any way you choose, or be able to treat yourself from time to time without worrying that you're ruining your budget. It might feel easier to order a pizza instead of slave over a hot stove to prepare dinner, but when that $20 for pizza isn't in the budget, it's accountability that will save the day.

When couples lack accountability in their finances, it leaves room for catastrophic consequences.

It's important to note that accountability is not a means for one spouse to control the other. When used properly, being accountable helps each of you to focus and stay the course in your journey to gain and maintain control of your finances.

Set spending boundaries and then lovingly help each other to stay within the means that you've collectively set for yourselves.

TALKING POINTS

Do you challenge your spouse? Or conversely, does it happen that any time your spouse says that they want to buy something that you go with it right away? It is important that you hold each other accountable and make sure both parties are following the budget. If you are not married, find someone that you can trust who will be brutally honest with you and hold you accountable when it comes to your finances to help you reach your ultimate financial goals.

CONCLUSION

Money and marriage are two topics that are tough to navigate in and of themselves. When you combine those two into one, then the level of difficulty is only increased.

It is well documented that one of the leading causes of divorce in North America is finances so it is imperative that you are proactive to prevent this from happening to you.

Opening the lines of communication within your marriage around the topic of finances is an essential component to your marriage being healthy.

Always keep in mind that communication is both the sending and receiving of information. We're blessed to have two ears and one mouth, meaning we should be striving to listen twice as much as we talk.

We pray that this book has allowed open and honest communication to blossom between you and your spouse. Just know that with consistent and effective use of these practices, you will begin to win with your finances!

ABOUT THE AUTHOR

Talaat and Tai McNeely are the real-life couple behind HisandHerMoney.com, a journey of how two high school sweethearts fell in love, got married, but were total opposites when it came to handling money.

Made in the USA
Middletown, DE
06 December 2015